Pyramids and Tombs

by Grace Hansen

DISCOVERING ANCIENT EGYPT

Abdo Kids Jumbo is an Imprint of Abdo Kids
abdobooks.com

abdobooks.com

Published by Abdo Kids, a division of ABDO, P.O. Box 398166, Minneapolis, Minnesota 55439. Copyright © 2024 by Abdo Consulting Group, Inc. International copyrights reserved in all countries. No part of this book may be reproduced in any form without written permission from the publisher. Abdo Kids Jumbo™ is a trademark and logo of Abdo Kids.

Printed in the United States of America, North Mankato, Minnesota.

102023
012024

Photo Credits: Alamy, Getty Images, Shutterstock, ©User:Master Uegly p7/CC BY-SA 3.0

Production Contributors: Teddy Borth, Jennie Forsberg, Grace Hansen
Design Contributors: Victoria Bates, Candice Keimig

Library of Congress Control Number: 2023937683
Publisher's Cataloging-in-Publication Data

Names: Hansen, Grace, author.
Title: Pyramids and tombs / by Grace Hansen
Description: Minneapolis, Minnesota : Abdo Kids, 2024 | Series: Discovering ancient Egypt | Includes online resources and index.
Identifiers: ISBN 9781098268473 (lib. bdg.) | ISBN 9781098269173 (ebook) | ISBN 9781098269524 (Read-to-Me ebook)
Subjects: LCSH: Pyramids--Egypt--Juvenile literature. | Tombs--Juvenile literature. | Tombs of the Kings (Egypt)--Juvenile literature. | Egypt--History--Juvenile literature.
Classification: DDC 932--dc23

Table of Contents

A Tomb for a God-King 4

Tombs through the Years 6

A New Era. 14

Terrific Temples 22

Glossary 23

Index 24

Abdo Kids Code. 24

A Tomb for a God-King

Ancient Egyptian pharaohs were god-kings. Only they could be certain of eternal life. Their tombs would help them get to the underworld after death.

Tombs through the Years

The first Egyptian royal tombs were called mastabas. They were low, rectangular buildings with flat roofs.

The pharaoh Djoser ruled Egypt during the Old Kingdom around 2650 BCE. Djoser was the first to build a new style of tomb, called the Step Pyramid.

Pyramid design improved over the years. Sneferu was the first pharaoh to use smooth sides. He built three different pyramids. The last, the Red Pyramid, was his best.

Sneferu's son, Khufu, built the most famous pyramid. The Great Pyramid of Giza stood 480 feet (147 m) tall. It took 2.3 million stones and 20 years to build.

king's chamber

air shaft
king's chamber
queen's chamber
entrance
chamber

13

A New Era

Building pyramids required a lot of **labor**. Pharaohs did not want to risk a **revolt**. So, they built smaller pyramids, **temples**, and **obelisks**.

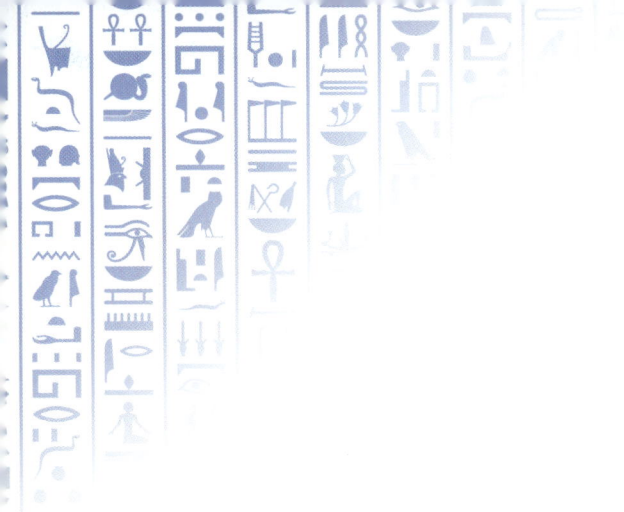

Pharaohs also used caves for tombs. These tombs were in a special place. This place is known today as the Valley of the Kings.

King Tut was one ruler buried in the Valley of the Kings. His tomb was discovered in 1922. It was filled with riches. It also held King Tut's mummy.

exterior

19

Nefertari is one of the best-known Egyptian queens. She was the **Great Royal Wife** of Ramses II. The grand tomb of Nefertari was found in the Valley of the Queens.

Goddess Isis

Nefertari

21

Terrific Temples

Luxor Temple

Temple of Hatshepsut

Temple of Karnak

Temple of Nefertari II

Glossary

eternal – having no end.

god-king – a human ruler believed to be a god or possess godlike powers or qualities.

Great Royal Wife – the honorary title that was used to refer to the principal wife of the pharaoh of ancient Egypt.

labor – hard work or effort.

obelisk – a tall stone shaft with four inclined sides and a pyramid-shaped point at the top.

revolt – to rise up and fight against the government or other authority.

temple – a place built for the official worship of the gods and in honor of Egyptian rulers.

underworld – also known as the Duat, the world of the afterlife where the dead roam. It is also home to several gods who help judge the dead.

Index

Djoser 8

Great Pyramid of Giza 12

Khufu 12

mastaba 6

mummy 18

Nefertari 20

obelisk 14

pharaoh 4, 8, 10, 12, 14, 16, 18, 20

Ramses II 20

Red Pyramid 10

Sneferu 10, 12

Step Pyramid 8

temple 14

Tutankhamun 18

Valley of the Kings 16, 18

Valley of the Queens 20

Visit **abdokids.com** to access crafts, games, videos, and more!

Use Abdo Kids code **DPK8473** or scan this QR code!